THIS BOOK BELONGS TO:

For
Roland
and Fi...

and
Imogen...

and
Giles.

HUBERT HORATIO
BARTLE BOBTON-TRENT
by Lauren Child
British Library Cataloguing in
Publication Data. A catalogue record
of this book is available from the
British Library.

ISBN 978 0 340 87789 0

Copyright © Lauren Child 2004

The right of Lauren Child to be
identified as the author and illustrator
of this Work has been asserted by her
in accordance with the Copyright,
Designs and Patents Act 1988.

Hardback edition published 2004
Paperback edition published 2005
10 9 8 7 6 5 4 3

'Monopoly', 'Boggle',
'Kerplunk', 'Twister',
'Cluedo' and 'Operation'
© 2004 Hasbro.
Used with permission.

Published by Hodder Children's Books
a division of Hachette Children's Books
338 Euston Road London NW1 3BH

Designed by
Lauren Child & David Mackintosh

Printed in Singapore
All rights reserved

HUBERT
HORATIO

BARTLE BOBTON-TRENT

LAUREN CHILD

h
*Hodder
Children's
Books*

A division of Hachette Children's Books

Mr and Mrs Bobton-Trent were frightfully, **frightfully** rich.

They lived in a large luxury house in London, a swankily swell house in New York and a marvellously marble house in Milan. They took trips here, trips there and trips everywhere you could trip to. They bought anything they could think of buying: rare rugs, tiny televisions, crocheted cushions, tailored trousers, plush pyjamas, abstract art, china curiosities, posh pets, pungent plants and strangely-shaped swimming pools.

They went out to dinner almost every night, for two, for twelve, for two hundred and two. They dined with the president, the prime minister and the queen. They knew simply everyone who was anyone. But, after a while, they began to tire of the same old places and faces and wanted to meet someone new.

So they decided to have a child.

Mr and Mrs Bobton-Trent were
delighted with him. They named him
Hubert Horatio Bartle Bobton-Trent.
Most people called him
Hubert Horatio Bobton-Trent for short,
or **Hubert Horatio** for extra short.

But his parents simply called him *H* because
they could never quite remember the whole thing.

Remembering things was not one of
Mr and Mrs Bobton-Trent's strong points.

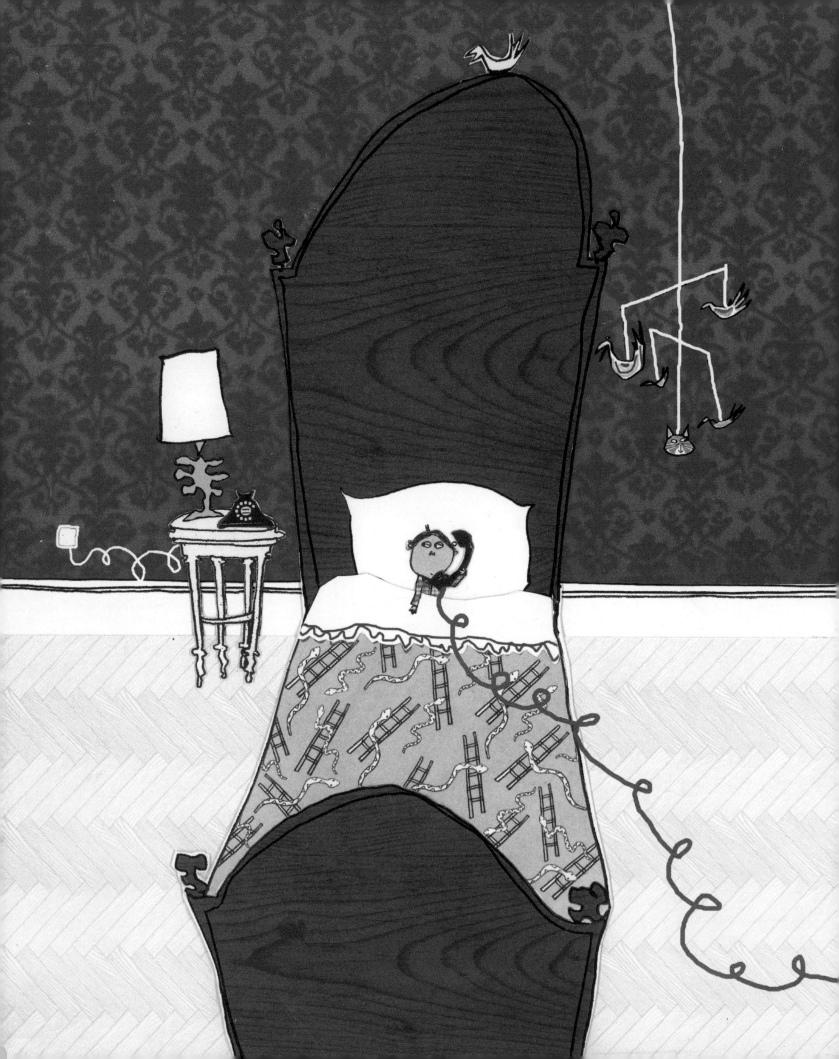

ONE day, when Hubert felt he was old enough to tell his parents that he did not like to be called **H**, he telephoned down to the drawing room where his parents were doing some light entertaining with the Elfington-Learies.

This was when everyone realised that the one-year-old Hubert could not only speak but could also use a telephone.

WHEN Hubert was two,
Mrs Bobton-Trent, unable
to find a blanket, tucked
him up under a copy of
The Whispering Weekly,
her favourite gossip journal.
Upon waking, Hubert
read the magazine
twice front to back and
once back to front.

This was when Hubert found
out he was a pretty good reader.

ONE year later, when the Bobton-Trents were engaged in a furious game of dominoes with their dear friends and next-door-but-one neighbours the Davenport-Martins, Hubert Horatio fell into the swimming pool.

This was when the three-year-old Hubert discovered he was a natural swimmer.

IN fact, Hubert Horatio Bobton-Trent
was a natural at almost everything –
with the notable exceptions of
cake baking and flower-arranging.

He really had
to work at
those two
skills.

HUBERT
very much enjoyed his
parents' company…

…and so every night

he would join them for cocoa by making

his way down three flights of stairs…

…left at the marble bust of Madame Marparcello…

His cocoa was
always a little
cold by the time
he got there.

…right at the *potted* palm…

up two flights of stairs and then three small steps to his parents' bedroom door.

…along the east-wing corridor…

USUALLY he found his parents playing Monopoly in their pyjamas.

They took the game very seriously and seldom played without real money.

All three Bobton-Trents were devoted games players and committed cocoa drinkers.

OVER the wall in the next-door mansion lived
the Saint Bernards – pronounced Ber-*Nard*,
emphasis on the Nard.

Like Mr and Mrs Bobton-Trent, the Saint Bernards also had one son who was a child genius.

Stanton Harcourt the third was exactly as bright as Hubert Horatio, so together the two of them were

He was called Stanton Harcourt the third and was Hubert's best friend and a keen table tennis enthusiast. probably the most brainy person in whatever country they happened to be in at the time.

HUBERT and Stanton Harcourt the third liked
to spend time concocting experiments and discovering
formulas in their home-made laboratory.

Sometimes, just for the fun of it, they would multiply
tricky fractions and then divide them by the square
root of a difficult digit. Other times they would quiz
each other on obscure Japanese vocabulary.

When *they* were not doing that they were playing table tennis.

ONE Tuesday, Hubert returned from school to find an invitation from his parents. It said:

Dearest H,
Are throwing an enormous party and inviting absolutely everyone we have ever met and some we haven't. Please join us in the ballroom.
With love,
your parents.

Hubert always enjoyed these parties as he was an exuberant dancer.

However, on this occasion something very odd occurred: halfway through the party, the jelly ran out.

This was highly unusual.

Hubert's parents never ran out of anything.

THE next strange happening
took place when Hubert and Stanton
Harcourt were on the roof counting
moon craters at dawn. They noticed
Mr Grimshaw the butler handing
the milkman a priceless portrait
of Mr Bobton-Trent's great-great-
grandfather in exchange for
two pints of milk.

A few evenings later, Mr and Mrs Bobton-Trent were entertaining the Butterworth-Trotters and eagerly waiting for Martha the maid to serve them their sautéed scallops. After nearly one hour and twenty-two minutes of no food appearing, Mr Bobton-Trent said, 'Where on earth do you think Martha has got to?'

Hubert Horatio quietly slipped off his chair and went to investigate.

IN the kitchen, he found Mr Grimshaw the butler eating cheddar cheese and stale bread.

Mr Grimshaw explained that, unfortunately, the chef had resigned due to lack of ingredients. Martha and all the other staff had left due to the fact that they hadn't been paid for at least two years, and that he himself would have to resign if he didn't get paid by nine o'clock the next morning.

The immediate problem of what to feed the guests was solved by Hubert, who was a creative chef and quickly rustled up cheese on toast for four.

Delicious.

After serving it to his parents and guests, he went off to his room to see what funds he had in his personal piggy bank…

THERE turned out to be
no more than a paper clip and
a slightly hairy cough drop.
It dawned on Hubert
that the Bobton-Trent
fortune was in
a very bad way –

i.e. there was none.

CLEVERLY,
Hubert managed to sell a
slightly broken table tennis
bat, an ugly bedside lamp
and some back issues of
The Whispering Weekly
over the phone to his
friend Elliot Snidge-Combe,
thus giving him enough
cash to pay Mr Grimshaw's
wages.

THAT night,
unable to sleep,
Hubert telephoned
his best friend and
algebra partner
for some
financial advice.

After some 5.33 minutes of calculations, Stanton Harcourt announced that the only sensible way out of financial ruin was to sell the Bobton-Trent family home. **Hubert Horatio was horrified.**

His parents loved their beautiful mansion. How would they cope if they ever found out they were no longer frightfully, frightfully rich?

What would happen to Grimshaw?

And in any case where would he put his table tennis table?

THE following day they both came
up with an ingenious solution.

They decided to enter

Mr and Mrs Bobton-Trent

in various games contests.

Hubert's parents were champions of

Chinese chequers,

and could beat anyone on the Scrabble board,

but Boggle was where they really excelled.

They

won

everything.

More often than not the Bobton-Trents would celebrate…

… taking *all* the other contestants out to supper.

IT was Stanton Harcourt who came up with the second brilliant plan. With Mr Grimshaw's help, the two boys sold tickets and the Bobton-Trent house was opened to the public.

WOBBLY GEORGIAN SIDE
TABLE SUPPORTING A
BOBTON-TRENT FAMILY HEIRLOOM
VALUE: PURELY SENTIMENTAL ➡

ROCCOCO CUCKOO CLOCK
ORIGIN: AUSTRIA
VALUE: EXTREMELY EXPENSIVE ⬅

Hubert's parents were astonished when suddenly their afternoon game of

ITALIAN MARBLE BUST
OF MADAME MARPARCELLO
ORIGIN: PISA
VALUE: MAMA MIA! ➡

VERY TALL VASE, SLIGHTLY CHIPPED.
(PRICELESS IF UNCHIPPED)

tiddlywinks was interrupted by a party of sightseers having a good old nose around their home.

SLIGHTLY LEAKY JUG
SHOULDN'T BE USED FOR
FLOWER ARRANGEMENTS

GRANDFATHER CLOCK
ORIGIN: HUBERT'S GRANDFATHER
IN GOOD CONDITION EXCEPT FOR
SOME SQUEAKING SOUNDS
(THE CLOCK, NOT HIS GRANDFATHER)

WOBBLY GEORGIAN
CARD TABLE
HEIGHT: FIVE HANDS

INDIA RUBBER PLANT
ORIGIN: CALCUTTA
VALUE: ABOUT ONE THOUSAND
PENCIL ERASERS

UNFORTUNATELY,
Mr and Mrs Bobton-Trent were
delighted by the unexpected guests.
So much so that they invited them
back the following week and,
of course, this added up to several
hundred people. And just tea alone
for several hundred adds up to
several hundred.

Before Hubert and Stanton
knew it, all the profit from
ticket sales had gone.

It seemed,
after all, there
was only one
solution.

IT was with a heavy heart that Hubert Horatio finally asked Grimshaw to drive himself and Stanton Harcourt to the estate agent.

After several nail-biting seconds the agent said that he might have a home that the Bobton-Trents could afford. It was excitingly called:

17b Plankton Heights. With great trepidation Hubert went home to tell his parents the unfortunate news.

IT WAS
PERFECT.

But what a
surprise –

Mr and Mrs
Bobton-Trent
liked it at
once.

For one
thing,
it had a
great view
and, for
another,
all the
rooms
were next
door to each
other.

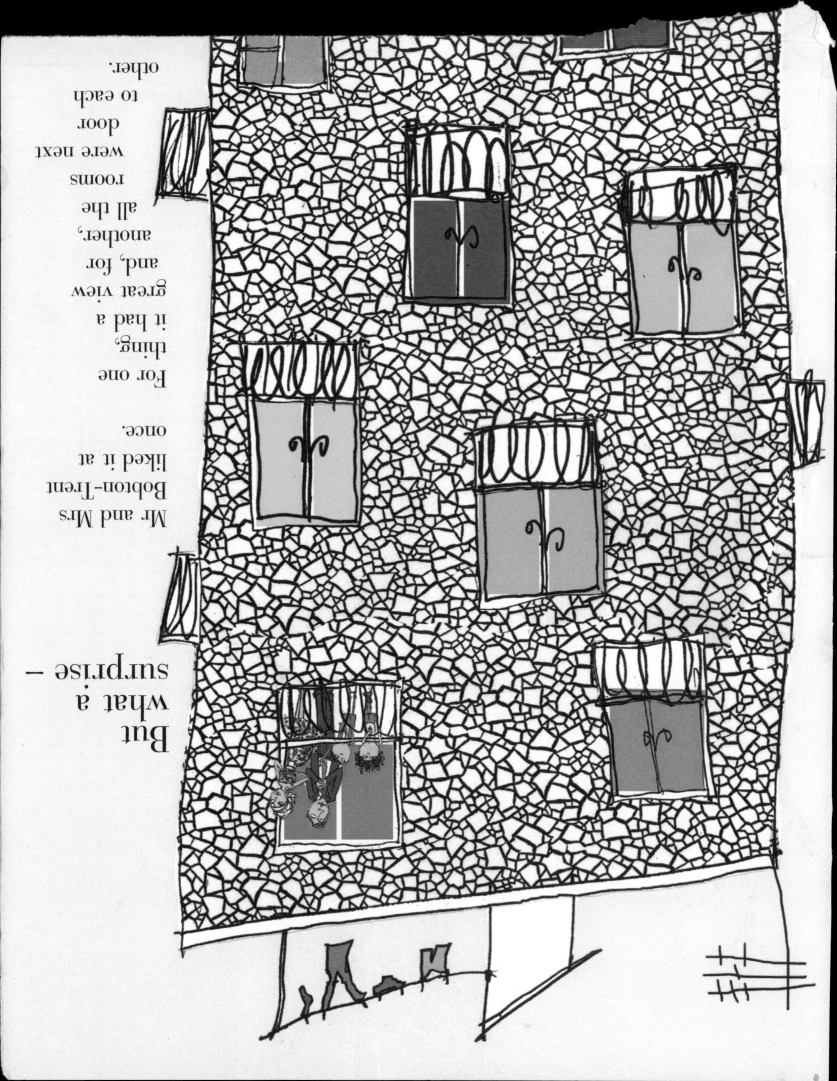

MRS Bobton-Trent loved that there was always
someone available for a game of Kerplunk.
Mr Bobton-Trent started his career as doorman,
a job perfectly suited to his social skills. Mr Grimshaw
retained his job of butler, taking care of all the residents.

And Hubert and Stanton Harcourt the third found
the perfect place for the table tennis table. Hubert's parents
said, 'Hubert Horatio Bartle Bobton-Trent, you are
a genius for moving us here. We have never been so happy!'

And Hubert realised that being frightfully, frightfully, frightfully rich was not frightfully important to his parents after all.

AND, for the first time ever, Hubert Horatio's
cocoa was still warm by the time he had
walked the short distance to his parents'
room to say, *'Goodnight!'*

On the outside, Girl is little.

On the outside, Dragon's biggle.

But they're *just* the same size

exactly the same size

in the middle.

Dragon makes a fire

    such a roasty, toasty fire

and he roars a dragon roar

    such a rum-below *roar*

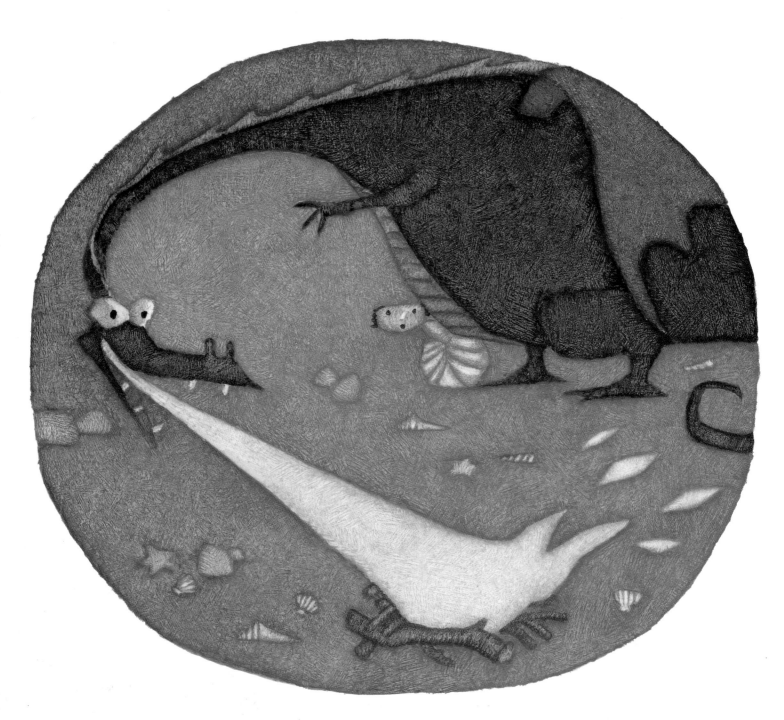

that the giants and the monsters never growl nevermore

and she's lonely for a dragon nevermore.

Now she sings little songs

little lovabye songs

and he wraps his tail around her

so gently, all around her.

Now they're friends.

Best friends.

For ever friends.

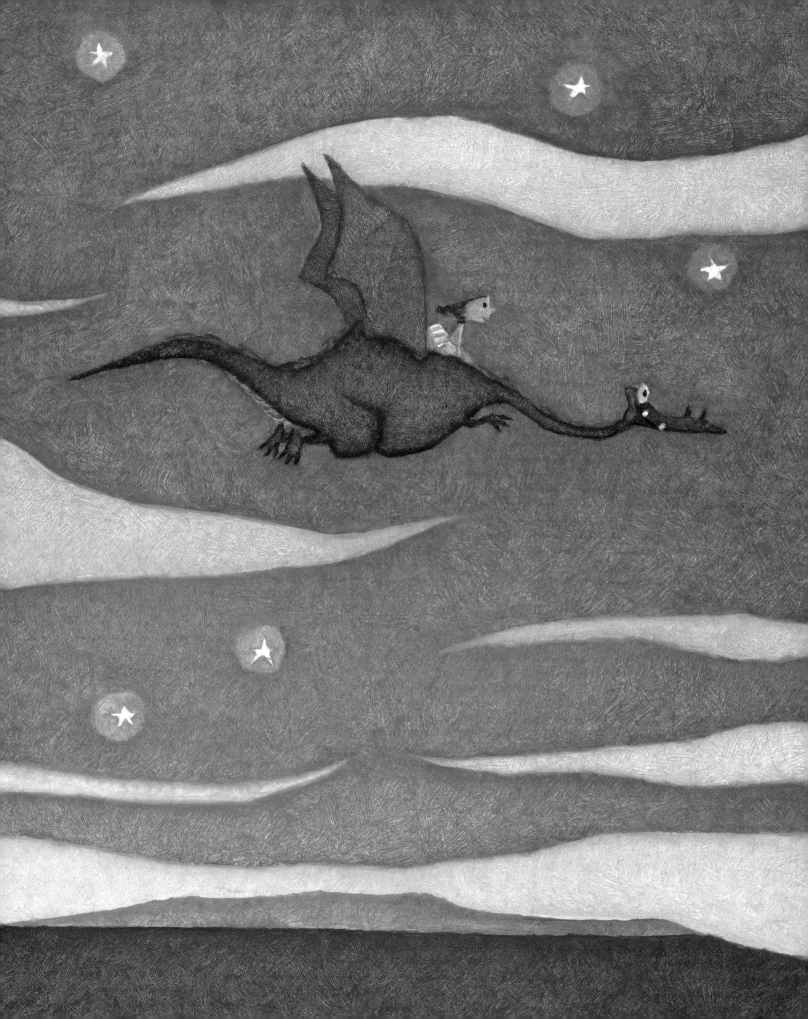

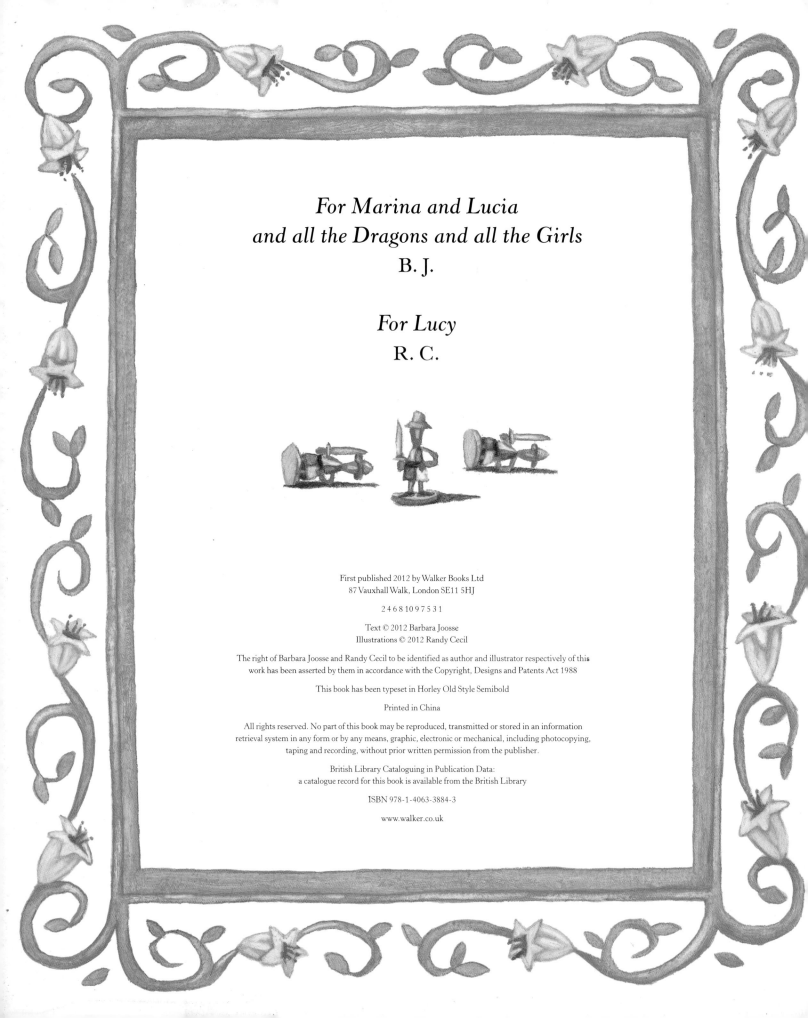

For Marina and Lucia
and all the Dragons and all the Girls
B. J.

For Lucy
R. C.

First published 2012 by Walker Books Ltd
87 Vauxhall Walk, London SE11 5HJ

2 4 6 8 10 9 7 5 3 1

Text © 2012 Barbara Joosse
Illustrations © 2012 Randy Cecil

The right of Barbara Joosse and Randy Cecil to be identified as author and illustrator respectively of this
work has been asserted by them in accordance with the Copyright, Designs and Patents Act 1988

This book has been typeset in Horley Old Style Semibold

Printed in China

British Library Cataloguing in Publication Data:
a catalogue record for this book is available from the British Library

ISBN 978-1-4063-3884-3

www.walker.co.uk